Making Wishes

Quotes, Thoughts, & a Little Poetry
for Every Day of the Year

Making Wishes

Quotes, Thoughts, & a Little Poetry
for Every Day of the Year

Written by
Richelle E. Goodrich

TABLE OF CONTENTS

Dedicated to my son, Philip
Go ahead, make a wish

Sometimes while gazing at the night's sky, I imagine stars looking down making wishes on the brightest of us.

~Richelle E. Goodrich

JANUARY

Determined, I rise
and face the dawn with resolve.
This time I will win.

January 1ˢᵗ

Today is the day that good things come
your way,
and then bad things to suck all the fun
from your play.

Today is the day that you stub every toe;
blow your nose on a sleeve thinking no
one will know.

Today is the day the sun bursts from the
clouds,
and sunbeams rain down as you smile and
sing loud.

Today is the day that you meet someone
new.
You'll tickle his fancy—he'll tickle yours
too.

Today you spend beaming; you'll sigh with a frown.
You'll buoy up all happy and cry when let down.

Today is the day you will figure things out, 'cause today is called *life* and that's what life's about.

January 2nd

A man once believed he could fly—and he did.
Another believed he could walk on the moon—and he did.
Why not believe your wildest dreams can come true?
Why not see the stars as reachable?

January 3rd

Sometimes the difference between success and failure is simply the degree to which you crave one over the other.

January 4th

Doing nothing accomplishes nothing, gains nothing, changes nothing, and wins nothing. You have to make a move.

January 5th

No one is born a sprinter. We all learn to push ourselves up from the floor and then balance before taking that first, wobbly step. It is an individual choice where to go from there.

January 6th

Today is a BRAND NEW day—a perfectly good reason to get up and start again. Never give up.

January 7th

You'll be hard-pressed to reach your goals if you don't map out where you're going. Take time to navigate your life.

January 8th

A little here and a little there will always accumulate, so why be surprised when steady, small steps take you to great places?

January 9th

Small steps may appear unimpressive, but don't be deceived. They are the means by which perspectives are subtly altered, mountains are gradually scaled, and lives are drastically changed.

January 10th

People will insist on building high and wide barriers directly in your path, often with the intent of closing you in. If you treat these obstacles like fencing walls, they will prove mightily so. I choose to see them as grand towers meant to be scaled and conquered, providing an added victory as well as a great view of the journey ahead.

January 11th

If you plan to build walls around me, know this—I will walk through them.

January 12th

Raging fires grow from the tiniest spark; it is the same principle at work in life. As long as there's a spark, tend to your fire. Never give up.

January 13th

Achievers are those who have redefined impossible, changing *what can't be done* into *a work in progress*.

January 14th

You stare at your dream from a distance, longing, sighing, seeing what you deem is a warning of IMPOSSIBLE. But if you'd squint real hard you'd see the truth; the sign correctly reads, 'I'M POSSIBLE.'

January 15th

The sun shines every day without being
told that it is brilliant. The mountains
stand tall and majestic though no one
informs them of their grandeur. The winds
twirl and dance with clouds, minus cheers
or compliments to inspire their moves.
Flowers bloom, showing off colors, long
before passing smiles acknowledge any
beauty. The ocean claps at its own
underwater chorus without topside ears
listening. What is the world trying to tell
you?
Be wonderful because you are.
Quit waiting to be told so first.

January 16th

Discouragement is like a scorpion in your
shoe; it takes courage to toss it out so you
can move on.

January 17th

Never give up.
This applies to more than goals and dreams, it is a maxim for basic daily struggles. It shapes one's life, including the will to continue to live. It supports love and committed relationships; it bolsters hope, faith, and charity; it is power in every area of existence. Never give up on anything or anyone of any worth, especially yourself.

January 18th

Trying again is okay. Trying again and again and again is okay. It's sort of an infinite thing because the alternative is failure, and that's *not* okay.

January 19th

I learn by doing....the same thing over and over and over again countless times.

January 20th

If I must start somewhere, right here and now is the best place imaginable.

January 21st

Do the small stuff. A consistent *little* will earn you *a lot*.

January 22nd

My goals may seem impossibly far-fetched when really they're not.
Break them down into steps and see how I accomplish great things.
I can easily reach from A to B.
I can manage from B to C.
I can then make it from C to D.
And so eventually, I will find my way from A to Z.

January 23rd

Words have less substance than air. Don't tell me about your zealous dreams, your firm convictions, your profound love—show me.

January 24th

The person *I am* and the person *I wish to be* are not the same. But if the gap between both decreases day-by-day, then it is okay.

January 25th

The key to success—keep swimming. Even when they tap you on the shoulder to say the pool has been drained, just keep swimming.

January 26th

Flames burn as long as they are fed.
Rivers rage as long as it rains.
The sun rises as long as the earth rotates.

Prayers are answered so long as they are uttered sincerely.
Hope exists so long as there is a new day.
Miracles never cease so long as there is faith.
Love endures so long as kindness rules all actions.
Dreams thrive so long as they are pursued.
Never give up.

January 27th

There are no real start-overs, only start-from-heres.

January 28th

Believing in yourself means more than simply believing in your own ultimate success; it means believing you will survive failures, disappointments, rejections, and criticism but still persist.

January 29th

Life requires more *doing* than *dreaming of doing* to make a dream reality.

January 30th

Life is the clay from which dreams are molded.

January 31st

Don't give up.
I know you've made a thousand attempts to reach your goal, but look at it this way: after repeatedly banging your head against the wall, you ought to be numb enough to break through this time.

FEBRUARY

A whiff of fresh mint
that tastes like strawberry pie.
Your kisses tempt me.

February 1st

Once upon a time there was a king and a queen though not of the same kingdom. They were of different lands and ruled over very different subjects, possessing unique talents and single hearts.

This valiant king and beautiful queen one day found themselves treading the same route which happened to meander through both their lands. Upon this chance meeting they detected in one another distinctive, worthy qualities, both intriguing and impressive enough to cause them to want to cross paths again.

Letters were exchanged from his kingdom to hers, delivered in haste. For even the heralds could see what a marvelous thing it might be to join these two great empires. And so, through written exchanges, it was agreed that this king would escort the queen in his grand, red carriage to view the celebrated, annual light festival in her land—an experience enjoyed after sunset.

On the night of the event, they rode along for hours, talking, laughing and smiling frequently at one another. Their hearts beat in rhythm, pattering with pleasure and tenderness, one toward the other. Jolly tunes played over the air, enhancing their bliss. The king shared pictures of his royal family and subjects, portraits that pleased the beautiful queen. And upon this enchanted night, surrounded by twinkling lights, their hearts swelled and the two fell in love.

It was not long before their kingdoms joined; a merger solidified through marriage. It was a union that made them both forever good and rich.

To say that they lived happily ever after would be in error, because their days consisted of continual and unnumbered trials. There were some periods that sparkled and warmed their souls like the festive lights under which this king and queen fell spellbound in love. Other times proved darker, but not without growth and gain. The promise was that through enduring these trials together—remaining a forever united kingdom in laughter, sorrow, hardship, and love—their uniquely beating hearts would eventually, someday, meld as one.

The Valentine is *one heart* shared by *two*.

February 2ⁿᵈ

You need tell me nothing; I already know your heart. Through your simplest choices you've given yourself away.

February 3ʳᵈ

I love you because you loved me first.
Yet you love me, saying I loved you first.
Funny, our love thrives believing the other person started it.

February 4ᵗʰ

What's the point of changing who you are in order to impress a woman, when your intention is to return to who you were, a person she was never attracted to in the first place?

February 5th

"When you do fall in love with me, I don't want it to be because I gave in to your demands, but because your heart gave in to its desire to truly be loved."

—from '*Eena, The Return of a Queen*'

February 6th

Love is many kind acts accumulated over time that leave us feeling wonderful.

February 7th

If only you would kiss me.
Press your lips to mine like a searing iron.
Wrap me in your arms as if you were a monarch claiming a kingdom. Hold me close until I warm through to the core. Do this, and I promise to melt into you, no longer a cold and frozen figure in your

narrowed sight. How devoted I would be
if only your lips burned for mine!
If only you would kiss me.

February 8th

It is a sweet thing to have someone love
you, but it is a far sweeter thing when his
actions convince your heart, and his words
persuade your soul.

February 9th

The search only ends when you finally
find the one who truly gets you.

February 10th

Life is a love story, with every character
yearning for permanent refuge in
someone's heart.

February 11th

To a man, sex is the ultimate expression of love. It is pure pleasure. But to a woman there exists something greater than pleasure—gestures of adoration. A gentle caress on the cheek, an attentive smile, a soft kiss while swept away in a slow dance, the whispered words, *'You're beautiful'*—these are the tokens of love that women cherish.

February 12th

They tell me you're the best and the worst thing to have happened to me, but I do not see how it can be both. For if my death resulted from your presence, an everlasting sleep would have me dreaming happily of us together. I see no bad in that. Therefore, you must be the best thing to have ever happened to me because you make the worst seem wonderful.

Love is an afternoon of fishing when I'd sooner be at the ballet.

Love is eating burnt toast and lumpy graving with a big smile.

Love is hearing the words, *'You're beautiful,'* as I fail to squeeze into my fat jeans.

Love is refusing to bring up the past, even if doing so would be a slam dunk to prove your point.

Love is your hand wiping away my tears, trying to erase streaks of mascara.

Love is the warm hug that extinguishes an argument.

Love is a humbly-uttered apology, even if not at fault.

Love is easy to recognize but so hard to define; however, I think it boils down to this...

Love is caring so much about the feelings of someone else, you sacrifice whatever it takes to help him or her feel better.

In other words, love is my heart being sensitive to yours.

February 14th

To the romantic soul, the rituals of Valentine's Day echo every day of the year.

February 15th

Though I love you to the core of my being, so thoroughly that every cell comprising me aches to be near you, I must accept that we can never be together. For our existence parallels the sun and the moon— a temptation in constant, beautiful view, yet if the sun were ever to kiss the moon it would devour the heavenly orb whole. Oh, my darling, if only I were the moon! Then I would dare taste your lips and be happy for my last and final joy! But alas, I am the sun, and I will not venture to destroy the one I love.

February 16th

I believe people are more inclined to do their best, not when they feel loved, but when they feel loved regardless.

February 17th

The communication block between men
and women:
Men—"Can't you *hear* what I'm saying?"
Women—"Can't you *feel* what I'm
saying?"

February 18th

I don't doubt that you think you love me;
what I doubt is your understanding of love.

February 19th

You are not my sunshine. Sorry. You're
more like a gust of arctic wind that bursts
in and blows out all the candles when the
door cracks open.

February 20th

Often we withhold our affections, waiting
first for love to be extended to us. The
irony is that we are loved for loving.

February 21st

I think I'd rather be liked than loved.
It just seems as if more criticism and
chastening is shown to those we love,
while kind manners and compassion are
reserved for those we simply like.
So, I hope you like me.

February 22nd

It was God who gave a man's rib to a
woman. But it is man who must learn to
give away his heart and never take it back.

February 23rd

It's too bad we're not all teddy bears. More
stuffing would only make us cuter and
cuddlier.

February 24th

Take time to laugh, to talk, to hug, and to
cry. These are the human relief valves.

February 25th

Laughter and love are their own forms of exercise meant to keep a body healthy.

February 26th

Let the giggles fill your mouth because nothing tastes as sweet as laughter.

February 27th

Giddy is a grin and giggles and that glint of goofiness in your gaze.

February 28th

Be loved for who you are, for everything that constitutes you. Be loved for your core beliefs, your strengths and weaknesses, your admirable traits and troublesome baggage. Be loved for *you*, because anything less is not love at all.

February 29th

Thousands of hopeful days came to naught
before this one.
This was a golden day. Never give up.

MARCH

Oh, mightiest wind,
wilt thou cease thy breathing in
and hold thy exhales?

March 1st

I wished upon the moon one night,
bewitched by how it shone so white.
While staring up with some excite my eyes
beheld a wondrous sight! The moon, so
lustrous and white, transformed into an
armored knight who caused me just a
moments fright when he jumped down
from such a height. No more a soft
celestial light, he was my lover, day and
night.

This caused the world a serious plight.
How harsh a sting and deep the bite
inflicted on the world, alright, to lose their
blackest-hour light.

And so I've come to set things right, to
offer up without a fight my lover wished
for one clear night. I hold him close. He

hugs me tight, then climbs again to heaven's height to glow a bluer shade of bright. I stare at my beloved knight, not wanting to be impolite, and in my heart with all my might I wish a wish that isn't right.

Now and then the world still spites a shadowless and moonless night when we steal softly out of sight to hold each other 'til daylight and share in lovers' true delight.

March 2nd

Sail through the good days, and on bad days pick a spot of blue sky to steer toward.

March 3rd

Life is a voyage across troubled waters where our days are often spent clinging to the top of the highest mast, scouting for a comforting glimpse of shore.

March 4ᵗʰ

The only ship you can truly steer in this ocean is the one you're sailing. Quit trying to alter the winds; harness them.

March 5ᵗʰ

It is a greater triumph for the fearful soul who tries and fails than for the fearless who succeed.

March 6ᵗʰ

Win or lose, good or bad, the experience will change you.

March 7ᵗʰ

I'm not asking you to walk in my shoes; I'd never wish my afflictions on anyone. But could you walk beside me on secure ground and reach to hold my hand?

March 8th

Obsessing over something that has jarred your world is called coping.

March 9th

Don't judge too harshly, for if *your* weaknesses were to be placed under your footsteps, most likely you would stumble and fall as well.

March 10th

We are all guilty of sin, error, and moments of sheer stupidity; none of us should be casting stones. The occasional arced pebble might be overlooked.

March 11th

Don't be fool enough to think you can know a person's character after a few moments of observation. *You can't.* You have no idea where his life began or how his saga has unfolded thus far. Only his present state can you witness. To judge him at a glance is like reading one page in an open book, believing it's enough to confidently recite the story from beginning to end. True, one page may tell you much, but not nearly enough to accurately critique a book or evaluate a life. So, either become his friend and learn his entire story, or refrain from commenting on a tale you know nothing about.

March 12th

Sorrow on another's face often looks like coldness, bitterness, resentment, unfriendliness, apathy, disdain, or disinterest when it is in truth purely sadness.

March 13th

Even among familiar faces, people often feel invisible and desolate, like an island in cold waters or a shadow apart from the crowd. Be the reason another never feels alone.

March 14th

Sit with me, and I'll not be alone.
Hold my hand, and I'll not feel alone.
Cry with me, and I'll no longer suffer
alone.

March 15th

Sometimes all you can do is hug a friend
tightly and wish that their pain could be
transferred by touch to your own
emotional hard drive.

March 16th

You cannot appreciate what you have
never experienced. Sadly, full
appreciation tends to come only after the
experience is past.

March 17th

Corned beef and cabbage and leprechaun
men.
Colorful rainbows hide gold at their end.

Shamrocks and clovers with three leaves
plus one.
Dress up in green—add a top hat for fun.
Steal a quick kiss from the lasses in red.
A tin whistle tune off the top of my head.
Friends, raise a goblet and offer this
toast—*The luck of the Irish and health to
our host!*

March 18th

Imagine if we were all magical
leprechauns, and every wish ever made on
a four-leaf clover obliged us to help others
obtain their wishes. Now imagine if
people simply lived like this were true.

March 19th

Those things that challenge the worst in us
tend to strengthen the best in us.

March 20th

The first real day of spring is like the first
time a boy holds your hand. A flood of
skin-tingling warmth consumes you, and

everything shines with a fresh, colorful glow, making you forget that anything as cold and harsh as winter ever existed.

March 21st

I love when the sun plays hide-n-seek for a few days because its invisibility often goes unnoticed. The world seems content that its presence behind the clouds is enough. But as soon as that brilliant sun jumps into the open sky once again—shining in full splendor—our closed eyes automatically turn toward it, and we bask beneath a warm and tender touch, grateful all the more that our glorious sun exists.

March 22nd

If you've put a smile on someone's face today, you've done more good than you know.

March 23rd

Happiness has two hands: one with strength for lifting up heavy hearts and a gentle hand for tickling.

March 24th

"I wish I could fly.
I wish I were rich.
I wish I had more time."

"But you can, and you are, and you do;
I wish you would open your eyes."

March 25th

Making a wish is fun to do.
Dreaming it out is much fun too.
Work, and your wish just might come true.

March 26th

Someday my children will look fondly on the annoying things I did and see them clearly as evidence of love.

March 27th

Easter is...
Joining in a birdsong,
Eying an early sunrise,
Smelling yellow daffodils,
Unbolting windows and doors,
Skipping through meadows,
Cuddling newborns,
Hoping, believing,
Reviving spent life,
Inhaling fresh air,
Sprinkling seeds along furrows,
Tracking in the mud.
Easter is the soul's first taste of spring.

March 28th

The sunlight whispers in my ear, his breath
a warm, sultry tease. I shrink and duck
beneath a tree. My eyes squint to scan the
horizon for a glimpse of the wind, but
there are no ashen ribbons or golden waves
in sight. He is missing.

Trickling, tinkling notes reflect loudly off
a chandelier of glimmering droplets. The
rain sings to me, and I shield my eyes,

admiring the song. Far off in my western view I expect to see snow, but the sun grows hot with jealousy, knowing this. He refuses my snowman a place to set.

My sight drops to search for the man in the moon. Normally he rises dripping wet from out of the lake, often pale and naked, supple and soft to my caressing gaze. On rare occasions he dons a pumpkin robe as luminous as fire. Today he is draped in silks of the saddest blue. My heart weeps as he steals up and away.

An army of stars in shining armor come to my aid, and they force the sun into the ground—a temporary grave. I am fed with a billion bubbles of laughter until I feel I will burst. But the stars will not stop giving, and I will not stop taking.

A kiss brands my cheek, and I turn abruptly to find my snowman. He landed safely in the dark. We hide from the man in the moon behind a curtain of flurries to dance on polished rainbows and feast on stars until I hear a fire-red growl. The sun claws its way out of the soil, and everyone scatters.

March 29th

While silently brooding, I am drawn to the start of a sweet melody that travels to my ear from afar. I smile, reminded that my heart can dance when my feet can't.

March 30th

Aging is a mortal term that my immortal spirit doesn't quite grasp.

March 31st

There are no rest stops on the road of life. Otherwise they'd be congested with traffic.

APRIL

Wilted or in bloom,
taking or lending daylight,
the world transitions.

April 1st

I contemplate a lot of things,
Like why the sky's a shade of green,
And how it is that lions fly
While birds with wings refuse to try.

It's strange how snowmen never melt,
And sweaty feet are sweetly smelt,
And how so commonly we see
Young hippos nesting in a tree.

I wonder how they get up there,
And why the world is mostly square,
And how huge every nose would be
If we had only one, not three.

I cannot guess why hills are flat,
Nor can I say why twigs are fat.
I do not know how mud keeps clean,
Or why small kittens act so mean.

And while I'm thinking all this stuff,
Consider black marshmallow fluff,
And how the rainbows twist and coil
Around the clouds down to the soil

Imagine if our teeth were white
I'd want to keep them out of site!
It's crazy stuff I see in dreams,
To contemplate so many things.

April 2nd

Rest assured, you make perfectly good nonsense. I understand you one-hundred-percent not at all.

April 3rd

Laughter isn't a sign of insanity but a shield against it.

April 4th

Life is mental; it's all about attitude. The majority of it is lived in your head.

April 5th

We forget that the sweetest joys are found in the simplest acts: hugs, laughter, quiet observation, basic movements, holding hands, pleasant music, shared stories, a listening ear, an unhurried visit, and selfless service. It is sad we forget a truth so elementary.

April 6th

Jesus Christ died to save us from our sins; we tend to concentrate on that merciful fact. But isn't it also true He lived to show us a lifestyle free from sin? So, wouldn't following in his footsteps be something like preventative medicine?

April 7th

I dreamed my shoulders held up the sky for a thousand hawks that squawked and cawed and beat their feathered wings against the hotness of the day. I supported their flight, watching and marveling, until sweat dripped from my body, and groans crossed my lips over fatiguing muscles.

Choosing to let the sky fall, I awoke.

My eyes opened to a cast of hawks gripping me in their talons. They supported my weight, hauling me high above the clouds through a blue expanse of heaven. And though they struggled—squawking and flapping wearily—never once did a single bird release its hold.

April 8th

You can believe what you've been told. You can imagine in vivid detail the things explained to you. You may even feel emotions assumed to accompany the related experience. But you absolutely *cannot* know something with any real degree of understanding until you've personally walked the road yourself.

April 9th

Acknowledge that some moments are just plain awful—desperate and gloomy and painful and miserable and nothing at all but anguish. No truthful, cheerful thought in the world will fix it. So let me cry awhile. Don't try to find a sunbeam where a shroud of darkness encloses me. Let me mourn. Then, after the storm, when the tears have run dry and my eyes choose to open, I will look for your rainbow of hope.

April 10th

Sometimes giving up feels like the easiest thing to do.
But then the easiest thing has never produced more than a garden full of weeds.

April 11th

Many people believe they have found the key to Heaven's gate, not realizing that there is no key hole. It is a barrier upon which you must knock. And I believe that

it is by our small and simple acts of
kindness that we find the gate left ajar.

April 12th

What is
the right tool,
the best option,
the choicest gift,
the winning hand,
the greatest relief,
the finest revenge,
the sweetest drink,
the perfect response,
the working solution,
the strongest medicine?
The correct answer is *kindness.*

April 13th

Be good.
See good.
Choose good.
It's a no-brainer.

April 14th

Kind words are salve to a cankered soul;
spread generously.

April 15th

Kindness is still the best antidote.

April 16th

Don't seek to be happy; let everyone else
chase after that rainbow.
Seek to be kind, and you'll find the
rainbow follows you.

April 17th

Happiness branches from the tree of
kindness, abounding with the fruit of sweet
smiles.

April 18th

Few realize how loud their expressions really are. Be kind with what you wordlessly say.

April 19th

Kindness is my weapon of choice.
My second is a Semmian dagger.

—a weapon from *'The Harrowbethian Saga'*

April 20th

Kindness wields a sword of light against the darkness.

April 21st

In someone's darkest hour your simple act of kindness may imitate the sunrise, and to sad eyes you become their only source of light.

April 22nd

Kind words and tender affections will not save me from this lake of woe and misery, but they may be enough of a buoy to prevent my drowning.

April 23rd

Kindness is a magical spell—performed by enlightened beings—meant to enchant hearts and lift weary souls that they might fly.

April 24th

When kindhearted people smile, demons shrink and turn away as if tormented by the gesture. But when those beautiful smiles are made to fade, every awful creature in the world stands surer. So do yourself and mankind a favor and smile BIG whether you feel like it or not.

April 25th

The most irresistible beauty is the radiant glow from a kind and gentle heart.

April 26th

Beauty isn't visible; I don't know why people think it is. Perhaps because at times there are physical manifestations suggesting beauty exists in a person, but don't be fooled. Beauty isn't the packaging, it's the treasure wrapped up inside.

April 27th

Dress yourself in the silks of benevolence because kindness makes you beautiful.

April 28th

The trait I regard most highly in a man is kindness. Thoughtful, consistent kindness. All other qualities—whether charming, witty, handsome, enterprising, powerful, seductive, or ingenious—wither in comparison to a truly kind man.

April 29th

Kindness is a girl's best friend.

April 30th

The sun rose and said to me, "Be a ray of sunshine for someone today."
The wind nudged at my back and said to me, "Blow a kiss to someone today."
The rain wet my cheek and said to me, "Dry a tear on a somber face today."
The soil fed grass at my feet and said to me, "Add pleasure to a life today."
The ocean washed ashore and said to me, "Calm the tempest of a troubled soul today."
The mountain trembled and said to me, "Soften a heart of stone today."
The moon lit the night and said to me, "Show the way with your simple giving."

So I went and did as they bid me do.

And the sun shone brightly on me.
And the wind caressed my face.
And the rain washed away my stains.
And the soil made a rose garden along my
path.
And the ocean carried me from shore to
shore.
And the mountain sheltered me from
storms.
And the moon smiled down on me.

I've come to realize I can never give
enough to recompense what I get in return.

MAY

I stumble and fall.
I weep and struggle to rise.
My mom feels it all.

May 1st

You think I read your thoughts, but it's
your eyes that speak to me. When they
glisten with moisture, I see a depth of
emotion stirring behind them. One tearful
glance begs me for a reassuring embrace.
When your gaze glazes over like a misty
morning, I know I've lost you to personal
cares. A sharp, narrow look will keep me
at bay while a wink and twinkle and the
flirty flutter of your dark eyelashes invite
my company. The strength and duration of
a stare gives your feelings towards me
away. And when those wary eyes dart to
avoid my notice, all of your hidden secrets
are betrayed.

May 2ⁿᵈ

Oh, how clearly I see your faults! Such distinctly highlighted flaws; it's as if the sun and moon mean to keep them illuminated in my eyes. My mind is quick to spell out a simple remedy for those defects.

But alas, poor me! My own faults—which I only assume to have because all do—are blurred and obscured by a mental fog. I've no eyes with which to gaze back at myself. The sun and moon refuse their illumination, and my mind offers no sure elixir but a complex recipe scribbled in foreign words I scarcely comprehend.

May 3ʳᵈ

Trying to fix the shortcoming of others while ignoring your own flaws results in little if no improvement—not to mention bitter feelings. Concentrating on personal growth sets a good example and results in the improvement of one life if not more.

May 4ᵗʰ

There is no such thing as constructive criticism. There is constructive advice, constructive guidance, constructive counsel, encouragement, suggestion, and instruction. Criticism, however, is not constructive but a destructive means of faultfinding that cripples all parties involved. Don't be fooled into thinking otherwise.

May 5ᵗʰ

The least effort is the feat most likely to be accomplished.

May 6ᵗʰ

At times we feel outnumbered in our attempts to improve the world—to brighten and beautify, to preserve and heal and do what's best for humanity. Selfless efforts can start to feel beleaguering, discouraging, even pointless with so little support. It is at these times I remind myself that I would rather be the last Good

Samaritan standing than to join the ranks
of selfish multitudes creating misery.

May 7th

Without you there would be no me.
I am everything reflected in your eyes.
I am everything approved by your smile.
I am everything born of your guidance.
I am me only because of you.

May 8th

Mothers were meant to love us
unconditionally, to understand our
moments of stupidity, to reprimand us for
lame excuses while yet acknowledging our
point of view, to weep over our pain and
failures as well as cry at our joy and
successes, and to cheer us on despite
countless start-overs.
Heaven knows no one else will.

May 9th

"A warm feeling fell over the boy. A mix of security and comfort, as if a blanket were wrapping its soft layers around his heart and nuzzling him snuggly. Gavin loved his mother, and he would be forever grateful to his father for protecting her. The whole mystery behind it made him itch with curiosity, however."

— from *'Secrets of a Noble Key Keeper'*

May 10th

Moms are life's number one cheerleaders without uniforms.

May 11th

I've yet to find another soul who believes in me with the same fervency as my mother.

May 12th

What a mother wants is to hold her babies when they're small and to be held by them once they've grown tall. It's empty arms a mother dreads.

May 13th

Mothers care in volumes of tears and earnestness of prayers and a depth of emotion others cannot fathom.

May 14th

MOM—Mistress Of Miracles

May 15th

Oh, yes I *can!*
I'm *not* sorry!
The answer's *no!*
I really *don't* care!
And I do *not* always have to have the last word!
No—*I don't*!

May 16th

Thank you, Mom, for the way you
managed yourself during the childish,
mean, selfish, insensitive, irresponsible,
unreasonable, hateful moments I put you
through. From your example I learned to
be patient, positive, kind, selfless,
sympathetic, reliable, sensible, and loving.
You have my endless appreciation.

May 17th

Teach me to sing and recite,
To whistle and jingle and strum.

Teach me to color and paint,
To sculpt and weave and create.

Teach me to sway and dance,
To tap and leap and twirl.

Teach me to laugh and giggle,
To tickle and play and pretend.

Teach me that life is beautiful.

May 18th

It is strange how in childhood it feels like tomorrow won't come until the end of forever, but in adulthood it feels like the end of forever could come tomorrow.

May 19th

There once was a mother-and-daughterly pair
Who both had an itch just beneath their long hair.
Each had a bur with the prickles attached
Under a belt at the mid of her back.

"Oh, daughter, please scratch at my itch, will you not?
And pluck out the bur—I would thank you a lot!"
"I can't," said the daughter, "My own bur does sting.
And try as I may I can't reach the darn thing!"

"Oh pain!" groaned the daughter. The mom cried, "Oh drat!"

As each strained to reach her own bur at her back.
"It prickles like needles! It tickles like feathers!"
But easing the scratch was a fruitless endeavor.

The daughter about gave a sigh of despair
When all of a sudden her prick was not there.
The itch too was gone with some scritches and scrapes
Applied by old fingers in arthritic shape.

The daughter, so grateful to feel such relief,
Turned 'round to her mother and plucked out *her* grief.
She scratched her mom's itch just as she had done hers.
Now neither has itches and neither has burs.

May 20th

It's a difficult thing having a heart made of glass; people don't seem to realize how easily it shatters. How often I've swept up

the pieces and carefully glued them back
together.

May 21st

A wish is the link between *what is* and
what could be. It is a vine woven into a
bridge between the two. Once complete,
the bridge is crossed and the wish then
turns into *what is* while a far distant *what
could be* becomes the catalyst for another
wish. So you see, life is nothing more than
a string of wishes connected by our own
handwoven bridges.

May 22nd

It is darkness that reveals the brightest
stars and most ardent wishes.

May 23rd

The actual secret to success: Be a better
friend today than you were yesterday.

May 24th

Life requires us to do things *anyway*,
despite what sort of fear or monster or
tragedy or suffering lurks behind that
anyway.

May 25th

Seemingly insignificant choices are like
seemingly trivial seeds. Once planted,
they root and grow and spread into
something tremendous. Imagine the
prickly weeds some choices amount to
over time and be careful not to plant them.

May 26th

Some parts of life are lived in the shadows
where the only sunlight you feel is the
light you pray for.

May 27th

Learn to look up now and then, just in case
a piano is falling from overhead.

May 28th

"Death was a quiet evil, unavoidable like the dark night and defenseless sleep and tearful sorrows. It had hunted her down and slithered close, wanting only to smother every last flicker of life."

—from *'My Aquarius'*

May 29th

Missing someone is the reverberating echo of everything beautiful about her—her laugh, her song, her touch, her smell, the power of her words, and the constant shadow that lingers on as her perfect image in your memory.

May 30th

Across from campus there's a wooden bench that sits beneath a cluster of cherry trees. From there one can look to the right and see a dignified university decorated with red brick and crème lattice. On the left, a new playground sits in the middle of a green park, popular among children who giggle and shriek as if silliness were their universal tongue.

I found the bench, my favorite reading spot, occupied that afternoon by an older gentleman in a black ball cap. The gold insignia above the bill was a badge denoting some military cavalry. His smile was a more powerful draw for my attention; he seemed to be enjoying the nice spring weather.

I took a seat on the far end of the bench, a couple spaces down from him. He appeared lost in thought when I glanced his way, mesmerized by the youthful scene taking place a distance out on the playground.

"So, what've you been up to today, son?"

I squinted at the man, a bit startled by his raspy voice, uncertain if his question was meant for me. There was really no one else within earshot.

"Um…" It was the most intelligent answer I could manage in my befuddled state.

The old man twisted his neck to look at my face. His wrinkled smile stretched even farther as he waited patiently for me to provide a better answer to his question.

I fumbled around with a physiology textbook and placed it in my lap.

"Well, I uh…" I thought back to the beginning of my day and rehearsed it for him. "I woke up late this morning and had to hurry to my seminary class—drove two miles on an empty tank of gas. Luckily my old Ford manages pretty far on fumes. Then, after class, I purchased breakfast from a vending machine before hustling to take a grueling calculus test."

"You a math major?" the man asked.

I shook my head. "No, sir, not really. Pre-med. But I'm good at math. My other classes are organic chemistry and human physiology." I lifted up the textbook in my lap as proof.

The old man nodded. "You a lucky young fella. A religious boy?"

I gestured affirmatively. "I wouldn't drag myself out of bed at five o'clock every morning to attend seminary if I wasn't, I suppose."

"I s'pose not," the man agreed. "Did you fight for your seat in that class?"

"Fight?" I repeated, confused.

"You pay for it?"

"Oh….no, no, no. Seminary's free of charge. Anyone can attend if they care to rise before the sun and sanity."

The old man chuckled, but I got the feeling it wasn't because he found me funny. Then he went on to make an announcement, pointing a finger at my nose as if it were important.

"That there religion—that's Andy Shindler's right arm."

I waited for an explanation, but none came.

"Oh," I finally breathed and opened up my textbook. There was a section on facial muscles I needed to read. Another odd question hit my ear before I could find the right chapter.

"Someone force you to go to school? They makin' you learn what's in that book?"

"Um, no. No, sir, I've always wanted to be a doctor. I *chose* to take this class." Again, a rigid finger was pointed at me.

"Hmm. That there choice—that's James Kennedy's legs, both of 'em."

I tried not to look at the man as if he were talking crazy, but….

"Oh," I nodded.

"And that there book—" His stern finger nearly reached to touch the colorful skull painted on the front cover. "—that's Donald Maccaby's left eye. Lost his left ear too."

"From a book accident?" I couldn't help but ask. I imagined a shelf in the library falling over, the edge hitting an unsuspecting man named Donald Maccaby in the face. Ouch.

The crazy old man chuckled again. He didn't answer me but kept right on talking.

"I call all this here Willy Whitman's." His pointing finger gestured to our surroundings, mostly to the campus at the right of us. I wondered then if the guy was lost.

"Sir, that's not Whitman College. It's the University of Washington."

The old man looked at me, smiling, staring patiently as if I were actually the lost one. But I attended classes in those buildings every weekday; I was quite certain of the name of my own university.

I'd about decided to bury my head in my book and ignore the gawking madman when his features fell. The smile that had appeared pinned from ear to ear collapsed, and his twinkling blue eyes glazed over, dull and sober. His next words were not that of a madman at all, rather those of a wise, seasoned soldier.

"Andy Shindler, James Kennedy, Donald Maccaby, William Whitman—they were all privates who years ago served overseas under my command. Those men made great sacrifices in war. Lost limbs and other body parts. In William's case, his life. Their sacrifices—their losses— paid for the rights you and I and all these here people take for granted. The right to religion and school and books and writin' and speakin' and makin' choices that freedom allows us to make. That's why every time I see a token of such freedoms, I think of my old friends. They *are* those freedoms, son. They spilled blood for 'em, so you may as well call 'em by their rightful names—Andy, James, Donald, William, Logan, Jacob, Ryan, Michael, and thousands more valiant soldiers. Don't you ever forget it."

My head bowed, humbled. I finally understood.

"I won't forget," I promised.

"Good boy."

The man's smile returned as bright as ever. I closed the pages lying open on my lap.

"Sir, may I ask your name?"

He seemed pleased by the request and immediately shared it with me.

"Henry Starr, First Air Cavalry."

I pointed to the throng of children twirling, jumping, and running on a green expanse of American soil without a care or fear in the world.

"That there indomitable spirit—that's Henry Starr."

May 31st

The effects of loss are acute and unique to each individual. Not everyone mourns in the same way, but everyone mourns.

JUNE

"Because," said a boy.
"Because why?" asked a young girl.
"Because I love you."

June 1st

Rare and precious moments, how I long to live with you eternally! If only your sweetness never ceased to touch my lips, and the flutters you evoke nevermore faded away. I dream of your arm extended immeasurably to keep hold of my reaching hand.

But Father Time, being a cruel master, will not grant such a wish.

And so I tuck you away as cherished memories, stored in a treasure box buried in my heart. And in times of solitude, I shall bring you out to view like rainbows.

Poetry is the wailing of a broken
heart—the etched sorrows of despairing
souls. These artful words are an
exclamation in rare colors expressed
noiselessly on parchment.

Poetry is the unheard cry of a flower,
wilting. It is a humble, lucent tear shed
with meaning. It is the lovely portrayal of
ugliness and the bitter edge of sweet.

Poetry speaks to the spirit by piercing
understanding. It interprets all senseless
truths—beauty, love, emotion—into
sensible scrawl.

Poetry is vague affirmation and
bewildering clarification. Like the most
poignant of emotions, we understand the
essence but cannot adequately do it verbal
justice, crippled by inherently weak
tongues.

A spiritual soothsayer, poetry is the closest
thing to expression of feelings unutterable.

June 3rd

A poet is simply an artist whose medium is human emotions. A poet chisels away at our own sensibilities, shaping our vision while molding our hearts. A poet wraps words around our own feelings and presents them as fresh gifts to humanity.

June 4th

The bigger the dream, the better the story.

June 5th

Stand tall on the summit after a tedious climb. Take in the remarkable scenery and the exhilaration of accomplishment. But don't pause for long; there are greater mountains to climb while you still possess the drive and capacity to do so.

June 6th

Reading...
Inspires,
Enlightens,
Nurtures,
Refines,
Educates,
Informs,
Transforms,
Persuades,
Challenges,
Engages,
Entertains,
Mesmerizes,
Captivates,
Gratifies,
Rewards,
Quiets,
And calms.
Granted, it won't get the dishes done,
But sacrifices must be made.

June 7th

Reality and fantasy are not two separate
spheres but one whole. They are like a
world's atmosphere—reality behaving as a

low front, fantasy a high front. Each
remains somewhat distinguishable and yet
they swirl and join, affecting and
manipulating the other. One cannot
perceive where reality ends and fantasy
begins, but life would grow stagnant and
die without the influence of both.

June 8th

Time machines, magic portals,
transporters, worm holes, flying carpets,
relocation charms—such things do exist.
They're called books.

June 9th

How crazy it would be
if the moon did spin
and the earth stood still
and the sun went dim!

How absolutely ludicrous
if snakes could walk
and kids could fly
and mimes did talk!

How silly it would be
if the nights were tan
and the mornings green
and the sun cyan!

How totally ridiculous
if horses chirped
and spiders sang
and ladies burped!

How shocking it would be
if the dragons ruled
and the knights were daft
but the fish were schooled!

How utterly preposterous
if rain were dry
and snowflakes warm
and real men cried!

I love to just imagine
all the lows as heights,
and the salty, sweet,
and our lefts as rights.

Perhaps it is incredible
and off the hook,
but it all makes sense
in a storybook!

June 10th

> The bulk of life is discovering who you are—and then reconciling that with who you wish you were.

June 11th

> This is me today, but take heed; it is not the same me as yesterday, and it will not be the same me tomorrow.

June 12th

> The irony of life: Realizing a lifetime is barely long enough to figure out how it should have been lived.

June 13th

> Your life is a personal lesson. For everyone else it is a loud example.

June 14th

From good examples we learn how to be.
From bad examples we learn how *not* to
be. An observant and willing student can
learn from any circumstance.

June 15th

"*I will do what I say I will do,*" tis the
motto of all grand and worthy souls.

June 16th

You can't make me be nice.
You can't make me be good.
You can't make me believe.
But your example, your kindness, your
patience and love will *affect me* perhaps
enough that eventually I may choose to do
those things.

June 17th

It is neither trials nor relationships nor
successes nor failures that define a man,

but the choices he makes while handling them.

June 18th

Fathers are…
The teeth on a saw,
The head of a nail,
The blades on a mower.

Fathers are…
The grit in a tumbler,
The cement in the pit,
The coin for the machine.

Fathers are…
The air in the tires,
The spring in the suspension,
The key to the ignition.

Fathers are…
the confidence in a dare,
The energy of a command,
The boots for the trail.

Tis true you might make things work without them, but not at all like they were meant to.

June 19th

Fathers...
Rise at dawn.
Stand up strong.
Fix and build.
Plow the field.
Carry the weight.
Work 'til late.
Encourage our dreams.
Provide the means.
Fight with might.
Defend what's right.
Protect the home.
Refuse to roam.
Forge the way.
Take time to play.
Spoil our moms.
Keep home life calm.
And all because
of selfless love.

June 20th

Southern DADDY—Dandy At Doin'
Diapers Y'all!

June 21ˢᵗ

We try so hard to instruct our children in all the right things—teaching good from bad, explaining choices and consequences—when in reality most lessons are learned through observation and experience. Perhaps we'd be better off training our youth to be highly observant.

June 22ⁿᵈ

Life is a harsh, twisted paradox.
On one hand, you wish for no pain or suffering or misery on anyone. Yet you hope to see your children grow into individuals of compassionate and kind character. And it seems that pain, suffering, and misery adequately humble an individual, cultivating empathy and understanding for others in similar plights. While a life of ease and comfort and pleasure often fosters extravagant and selfish habits, spurring pride and blinded vision. Still, you pray for no pain or suffering on your children.
Life is a harsh, twisted paradox.

June 23rd

Far more important than the tribulations
and heartaches, the thrills, merriment, and
pleasures of life is what you learn from it
all. It isn't the tunnel we pass through that
matters; it's what emerges on the other
side.

June 24th

Patience isn't tested when it is self-
imposed and the duration is self-regulated.
Patience is hardly tested when the outcome
means little to you. However, when
circumstances beyond your control force
you to wait with baited breath knowing the
outcome will affect your life substantially,
that is the true test of patience. It is a cage
inside a burning building where every exit
is blocked by angels calmly advising you
to wait a moment longer. Your choice is
to either trust the messengers or madly
claw through them.

June 25th

Teddy bears, not grizzly bears, get invited in for honey.

June 26th

There are hundreds of reasons to be kind, but only one that matters—because it's who you are.

June 27th

Dogs are loyal friends, and if they could talk, your secrets would still be safe. (If my cat could talk, I'd have to let the dog eat her.)

June 28th

It's advice, not a commandment.
Don't swallow it whole until you're absolutely sure you've been given healthy advice.

June 29th

They say to never look back.
But sometimes I do.
It's gratifying to see how far I've come.

June 30th

In the middle of a grocery store, two children were horsing around (one holding the other in a headlock) when the mother turned abruptly to give them a stern reprimand.

"You two are old enough to know better than to behave this way in public! Could you—at least for the time we're in this store—mind your manners enough to *act like an adult?*"

The children took less than a moment to consider their mother's question before facing each other and engaging in the following conversation:

"I hate you."

"I hate you too."

"Let's get a divorce."

"Okay."

Perhaps '*act like an adult*' isn't such good advice anymore.

JULY

The blue of daylight
fades and chills as the sun sinks
beneath clouds of fire.

July 1ˢᵗ

Freedom is essential to the pursuit of
happiness.
Freedom is essential to artistic evolution
and expression.
Freedom is essential to the expansion of
the human mind.
Freedom is essential to the development
and application of basic humanitarianism.
Freedom is essential to the creation of an
individual's will, motivations, preferences,
and unique talents.
In essence, freedom is essential to the
success and progress of humanity.

July 2ⁿᵈ

Freedom is the atmosphere in which
humanity thrives. Breathe it in.

July 3rd

Years ago, a group of good, wise, brave, God-fearing men stood up to claim and defend the human right for independence. Those men are now dead. Their work is not. But if good, wise, brave, God-fearing men fail to stand up in their stead, that independence will cease to exist.

July 4th

Some say freedom is a **gift** placed in our hands by our forefathers.
Some say freedom is a human **right** that none should be denied.
Some say freedom is a **privilege** that can and will be seized if taken for granted.
Some say freedom is the **key** that opens doors otherwise meant to imprison.
Some say freedom is **power** to do, to be, to say, and to accomplish what the oppressed cannot.
Some say freedom is a **responsibility**—a weight to be carried and shared by those willing to protect it.

Perhaps freedom is all these things.

But in my eyes, I see freedom as a **treasure**. It is a gem so rare and precious, the fiercest battles rage over it. The blood of thousands is spilled for it—past, present, and future. Where true and unblemished freedom exists, it shines with perfect clarity, drawing the greedy masses, both those who desire a portion of the spoils and those who would rob the possessor of the treasure, hoping to bury it away.

Without freedom I am a slave in shackles on a ship lost at sea.

With freedom I am a captain; I am a pirate; I am an admiral; I am a scout; I am the eagle souring overhead; I am the North Star guiding a crew; I am the ship itself; I am whatever I choose to be.

July 5th

I once thought it would take a miracle to improve my circumstances. Now, I believe it will take something far more powerful, if such a thing exists.

July 6th

Powerlessness is an excruciating pain; it is torture insurmountable.

July 7th

When you reach the point you truly want someone to stop and listen, to hear even your unspoken words, to feel your depth of sorrow, to care unreservedly, and to completely understand—*pray*.

July 8th

The further you descend into a pit, the darker things appear. You can't keep digging to find the light.

July 9th

The key to a better life isn't always a change of scenery. Sometimes it simply requires opening your eyes.

July 10th

There are in this world ample reasons to be sad and disheartened, discouraged and fearful. But there are as many reasons not to be.

July 11th

The road to happiness starts with a deep breath and an awareness of the many blessings tied to that single breath.

July 12th

There are still blue skies and rainbows and days bathed in sunlight.
There are colorful shade trees filled with sweet bird songs.
And there are wishing stars in the heavens as well as angels in God's service.
So lift up your eyes.
Refuse to be unhappy.

July 13th

You're right; you can't *make* someone be happy. But I don't see the harm in trying.

July 14th

I can't force your lips to smile, but I can show them how easily mine do.

July 15th

Happiness must be a jealous pet. When you try seeking yours out, it tends to keep hidden. But as soon as you turn to help a friend find his, your own happiness comes bounding out of the darkness like some crazed animal.

July 16th

Life is hard and unfair. It is cruel and heartless, painful, trying, disappointing, unapologetic, and frequently downright awful. But that's not important. What's important is that through it all you learn how much you need your Heavenly Father and how much your friends need you.

July 17th

I've had the kind of bad day no quote can fix.

July 18th

One of the most critical decisions made in life is choosing with whom to spend your time. For it is those close relationships that gradually mold our character until we become a reflection of the company we keep.

July 19th

Friends are those crazy people who keep coming back, in spite of being exposed to the real you.

July 20th

Friendship is not about ships—no matter how big and fancy and expensive the yacht is.

July 21st

Choose altruism, because selfishism is a lonely, cold, dark hole.

July 22nd

True friends esteem you of greater worth than you feel deserving.
False friends demand you prove that worth.

July 23rd

People are drawn to you because you make them feel happy; I understand that. But wouldn't it be nice to have people flock to you wishing for your happiness?

July 24th

Be someone's security blanket when theirs is in the wash.

July 25th

I wish everyone had someone who never popped their balloons.

July 26th

Happiness is a simple game of lost and found: Lose the things you take for granted, and you will feel great happiness once they are found.

July 27th

I don't understand why when I wish for happiness it inevitably rains. However, I do tend to find myself grateful for sunlight once the storm ceases.

July 28th

It is the image of physical brawn, sheer force, and commanding volume we so often associate with might. But I have found the might of an army exists in the faith of a child and in quiet, earnest prayers as well as in the heart of one who loves.

July 29th

If there weren't so many interesting conversations taking place inside my head, I might venture to speak out loud.

July 30th

I looked out the window on an early-morning bus, noting how low the gray cloud-cover hung. The dark and heavy sky was threatening rain. I watched a tall line of trees that bordered acres of hay field, the wind flailing branches like they were bits of straw.

"What a miserable day," I sighed.

Surprisingly, someone responded to my bleak announcement—a man one seat back. "You just need new glasses," he said.

His hand reached over my shoulder, a finger and thumb pinched as if holding the thin arm of actual frames, only there was nothing in his fingers.

I glanced backwards, my expression questioning his comment as well as his sanity.

"Go on," he urged, holding up his gift of nothingness. My eyebrows slanted, appraising him.

"There's nothing there," I finally pointed out.

"Sure there is," he insisted. "These are *special* eyeglasses. Go on, put them on."

I played along, partly to be kind and partly to avoid a public scene with a madman. In a careful gesture, I took the invisible spectacles and pretended to slip them over my nose. Another rearward glance found the man smiling. He pointed at the window.

"Now look again."

My head turned the other way to take a second glimpse at the gray sky. There were raindrops clinging to the window now, tracing a slow, horizontal line across the glass. Before I could say anything, the man made a soft but excited observation in my ear.

"See that beam of sunlight streaming through the break in the clouds?"

It was beautiful, like a spotlight glimmering on a distant rooftop.

"And look there," he said, gesturing again at the sky. "See that rainbow? Or half of it, anyway."

My eyes followed a translucent smear of colors to somewhere behind a neighborhood of houses. I hadn't noticed it earlier.

"See those pink blossoms on that little tree?"

I nodded as we past it by. "Pretty."

"See the hawk circling right above it?"

"I think that's a blackbird," I said. It appeared charcoal from beak to tail.

"Huh…" He laughed for half a second. "That's one big blackbird!"

He gestured to an upcoming cluster of young evergreens growing tightly together on someone's property. "See the naked Christmas trees?"

Funny. It made me smile.

"Oh look!" I exclaimed, startled by my own unexpected exuberance. "Puppies!" I pointed at two young golden labs on leashes. They seemed more interested in wrestling one another than being walked.

"I see, I see," the man grinned.

He continued on, pointing out things beyond our window that were exactly opposite of the gloomy and miserable picture I'd beheld earlier. It amazed me the number of wonderful things he managed to find. Before long, I was noticing pleasantries he missed as we drove along.

Realizing the gift he'd given me, I thanked him. "I guess it's not such a miserable day after all.

He pretended to take back his lenses and smiled wide. "It's all in the glasses."

July 31st

Every person sees the world through lenses of his or her own design—individual goggles that alter focus and perspective as desired. For those who wish the world to be dark and ugly and unapproachable, it is. But for those who wish it to be beautiful, it is a garden playground blooming with bright, happy colors.

AUGUST

Compliments land as
soft and gentle on my ears
as a butterfly.

August 1st

What is this thing of intangible substance
that wreaks consequential havoc on our
lives? What is this sensitive thread that
runs through heart and mind, and when
given the slightest tremor grasps hold of
all sanity, dragging the afflicted down to
insufferable depths or flinging him
weightless to euphoric heights? What is
this magic we would deem imagination,
fantasy, or pretend if not for the evidence
of power manifest by human
consequences?

Effortlessly controlling us, it affects the
infected in an instant. It takes but one
word, one thought, one act to become
immersed.

To stop it is hopeless.

To stifle it, demanding.
To think to master it is both improbable
and pretentious.

What is this invisible hand that blinds our
eyes and dangles hearts by a string? It is
nature's drug and poison we call emotion.

August 2nd

There would be no cloud-nine days
without rock-bottom moments left below.

August 3rd

One thing about a skunk—once you
recognize the markings, you know things
are gonna stink.

August 4th

From the beginning, man could look up at
a vast universe dotted by innumerable stars
to find every evidence that he was nothing.
This evidence has only grown stronger as
science and technology record an expanse

of galaxies filled with planetary solar systems beyond any visible end. Man is but a grain of sand lost on an endless seashore, and yet he believes with conviction in his own greatness. He is either a divine soul intuitively aware of his inherent, limitless potential—or he is a blind fool.

August 5ᵗʰ

Your life isn't some prerecorded movie where, no matter how many times you watch it, the ending remains the same. Your life is a book in progress, and you are the author. So if you don't care for the main character or the gloomy scenery or how the twisted plot is unfolding, then do something to change it. *You write your own story.*

August 6ᵗʰ

This day is the most recent set of events to define you.
Every day changes your life. Every last one.

August 7th

Your problem is in thinking the sky's the limit. Why set limits?

August 8th

It's okay to be absurd, ridiculous, and downright irrational at times; silliness is sweet syrup that helps us swallow the bitter pills of life.

August 9th

"Reality depends a great deal upon one believing what he sees—or seeing what he believes. Either way."

—from *'Secrets of a Noble Key Keeper'*

August 10th

A first impression works like a magic mirror; it reflects what intrigues us rather than echoing a truthful picture. A first impression is the creating of an imagined character born from personal desires, perceptions, and biases. Though sparked by an introduction to a real, living, breathing individual, the person remains a mystery long after parting. It is a fictitious ghost masked with similar features that remains. A first impression is rarely accurate; therefore, it should never be trusted.

August 11th

Reality is a background so painted over by our own perceptions that every eye sees the world differently.

August 12th

Life is not what happens to us; it is what we perceive has happened to us.

August 13th

I'm generally quite happy until someone tells me I'm not. I don't see how they know I'm not, but suddenly I feel less happy.

August 14th

You made me laugh at your jokes.
You made me cry at your criticism.
You made me shout at your lies.

Then I noticed how in every case someone
else was present,
hearing you without laughter or tears or
anger.

I alone reacted.

I see now; you never made me laugh or cry
or rage.
I chose to find humor.
I chose to take offense.
I chose to feel scorned.

The truth is, you never had power over me.

August 15th

People are more inclined to ask *what's
wrong* than *what's right*. They note errors
and faults, seeing weaknesses before

strengths. So expect criticism; it's the nature of the beast.

August 16th

Your tongue tends to say more about you when it blabs about other people.

August 17th

If one is content to freely speak trash about another, it is probably more correct to judge them as the one of ill repute and refuse the load of garbage they offer you.

August 18th

"*I'm sorry*" won't fix what's been broken. It can't reverse time or undo the damage or change anything that happened. But a sincere, humble apology can serve to soften the sting and sometimes do a pretty good patch up job.

August 19th

Never believe you're so great or important, so right or proud, that you cannot kneel at the feet of someone you hurt and offer a humble, sincere apology.

August 20th

Your opponent's wrong doesn't automatically make you right. Most fights aren't about who's right; they are contention over degrees of wrongness.

August 21st

Saying *"I'm sorry"* is saying *"I love you"* with a wounded heart in one hand and your smothered pride in the other.

August 22nd

A sincere and warmly-expressed apology can produce the same effects as morphine on a suffering soul.

August 23rd

Be the hero of hearts; learn to say *I'm sorry.*

August 24th

A truly humble apology works to part storm clouds, calm rough seas, and bring on the soft lights of dawn. It has the power to change a person's world.

August 25th

Words never fade away but echo on for eternity. Let your echo ring sweet.

August 26th

Who cares who's right or wrong when the last word is a kind apology?

August 27th

Forgiveness is a revolving door positioned in your path. You must step through it to move on, but it takes both timing and decision to escape walking circles inside.

August 28th

How insane we are as humans when having received a nasty offense we return the same awful offense. If given an apple found to be rotten and wormy, would we not toss it aside rather than force a soul to eat it? Offenses should be discarded, not returned.

August 29th

It is an incapacitating emotion one feels upon hearing the whispered words *"I still love you"* after deeply hurting that soul. Forgiveness isn't weakness.
It is power.

August 30th

It is a difficult thing—if not
impossible—to forgive oneself for foolish
errors, not for trampling a life or goring
another with sharp horns, but for being the
fool who opened the gate and let the bull
out, blind to potential consequences.

August 31st

Very often, what is meant to be a stepping
stone turns out to be a slab of wet cement
that will harden around your foot if you do
not take the next step soon enough.

SEPTEMBER

At night I look up.
Mister Moon winks down at me,
and we exchange smiles.

September 1st

Pastel colors reflect in my opening eyes and draw my gaze to a horizon where the waters both begin and end. This early in the day I can easily stare without blinking. The pale sea appears calm, but it is stormy just as often. I awe at the grandeur, how it expands beyond my sight to immeasurable depths. In every direction that I twist my neck, a beauteous blue is there to console me.

Flowing, floating ribbons of mist form on these pale waters. In harmony they pirouette, creating a stretch of attractive, soft swirls. *Swoosh!* The wind, its strength in eddies and twisters, smears the art of dancing clouds, and the white disperses like startled fairies fleeing into the forest. Suddenly, all is brilliant blue.

The waters calm and clear. It warms me. Pleases me. Forces my eyes to close at such vast radiance. My day is spent surrounded by this ethereal sea, but soon enough the light in its belly subsides. Rich colors draw my gaze to the opposite horizon where the waters both begin and end. I watch the colors bleed and deepen. They fade into black.

Yawning, I cast my eyes at tiny gleams of life that drift within the darkened waters. I extend my reach as if I could will my arm to stretch the expanse between me and eons. How I would love to brush a finger over a ray of living light; but I know I cannot.

Distance deceives me.

These little breathing lights floating in blackness would truly reduce me to the tiniest size, like a mountain stands majestic over a single wild flower. I am overwhelmed by it all and stare up, in love with the floating sea above my head.

September 2nd

We wait for the rains to cease, the clouds
to part, and the sun to shine before saying
life is good. Ironically, it is because we
endure the storms that life seems so
wonderfully bright at their passing.

September 3rd

Pray each morning and each night.
Talk to God and be polite.
Tell Him what you're grateful for.
Leave your troubles at His door.

Share your wishes, needs, and hopes.
Ask God how to bravely cope.
Tell Him all you learned today.
Say the things you need to say.

Beg forgiveness for your sins.
Pray to live with Him again.
Speak with earnest heart and soul.
He will listen. This I know.

For prayer is hope put to the test.
And hope is faith in what is best.

Faith is power to do great things.
Thus, prayer is faith's enabling wings.

September 4th

God invites while the devil pressures and shoves and bullies. Realize who holds the actual power before you react. *You* are greater than Satan; *God* is greater than all.

September 5th

You stand a better chance of bringing pretend to life through the power of belief than you stand any chance of erasing what's real by refusing to believe.

September 6th

Imagine fantasy and pretend as neither fantastical nor pretended.....and then believe it.

September 7th

When I say I love the silence, I'm not
being entirely truthful. What I actually
love are the abundant, delicate sounds that
amplify when I'm silent. These curious
creaks, mutters, and hums compel my
imagination.

September 8th

I survive on moments of make-believe
happiness.

September 9th

Daydream. Because you can't accomplish
what you've never fully imagined.

September 10th

It's mind-boggling how many different
worlds people live in on this one planet.

September 11th

I opened my eyes today to a world that felt alien. For though things resembled the familiar, nothing was the same. Walls I once considered confining, crumbled at the slightest shove. Mountains that for ages had barred my view now faded, transparent. Meandering roads stretched out as straight as an arrow, void of stop signs. Obstacles no longer stood stationary. Pinnacles loomed within reach. Beasts were tame, bullies timid, wagging tongues all tied into knots, and in the palm of my hand glistened the end of a glorious rainbow. It took but a moment to realize that in my newfound sight, everything I'd ever longed for was accessible. Incredibly, the only thing that had really changed was the way I saw the world.

September 12th

I dream of defeating tyrants and ogres as well as circumstances and consequences that I cannot conquer in life. I dream of a love as sweet and addictive as chocolate-coated rose petals yet as tenacious as a thirsty vampire and as enduring as immortality. I dream of things improbable and boldly insane.

September 13th

Dreams become reality once the dreamer goes beyond imagining and acts them out.

September 14th

Relax; the world's not watching that closely. It's too busy contemplating itself in the mirror.

September 15th

The sun, rising and setting in splendid colors, never grows tired of its admirers—much like a lady, aglow with grace, never grows tired of chivalrous acts or pretty flowers.

September 16th

I like bubbles in everything. I respect the
power of silence. In cold or warm weather
I favor a mug of hot cocoa. I admire
cats—their autonomy, grace, and mystery.
I awe at the fiery colors in a sunset. I
believe in deity. I hear most often with my
eyes, and I will trust a facial expression
before any accompanying comment. I
invent rules, words, adventures, and
imaginary friends. I pretend something
wonderful every day. I will never quit
pretending.

September 17th

Those things that inspire, enthuse, and
compel you should consume your life.

September 18th

If you love something, you find a way to
have it in your life. Opposers may take
away your means and tools, but you
simply turn to crude replacements,
fashioning them from scraps if necessary.

Threats only make you steal moments of secrecy to satisfy your love. And if it means but a morsel here and there, you accept each crumb gladly because nothing else can even begin to satisfy your hunger.

September 19th

You made a choice—a single choice. How neat to think you may have opened the door to a wondrous future without knowing.

September 20th

Maybe not here and now, but somewhere, someday.

September 21st

Always be good, but be wickedly beautiful.

September 22nd

Autumn is a cunning muse who steals by degrees my warmth and light. So distracted by her glorious painting of colors, I scarcely realize my losses until the last fiery leaf has fallen to the ground and the final pumpkin shrinks. Autumn departs with a cold kiss, leaving me to suffer the frigid grasp of winter in prolonged nightfall.

September 23rd

Announcing the intended arrival of some people is kind of like issuing a hurricane warning.

September 24th

Life is a bonfire where everyone else has brought marshmallows, and you—a stick.

September 25th

> If only I could see myself from the same vantage point that I observe the world; I might judge my behavior and expressions more critically, and others less.

September 26th

> We change when circumstances necessitate it; we adapt because we have to. The real challenge is to change when circumstances don't demand it at all.

September 27th

> "You try moving things with nothing but willpower. It's about as easy as trying to lasso a bull with a licorice whip."
>
> —from *'Phantom's Veil'*

September 28th

> My favorite quote in the world is this one.

September 29th

Laughing in my ear is a muse amused by
how I paint her whims on paper with silly
words.

September 30th

Who told you it was too late? And more
importantly, why did you choose to
believe them?

OCTOBER

A finger beckons.
My choice is to turn away.
It is a mistake.

October 1st

You would never take a rose from a beast.
If his callous hand were to hold out a
scarlet flower, his grip unaffected by
pricking thorns, you would shrink from the
gift and refuse it. I know that is what you
would do.

But the cunning beast will have his beauty.

He hunts not in hopeless pursuit, for fear
would have you sprint all the day long.
Thus, he turns toward the shadows and
clutches the rosebud, crunching and
twisting until every delicate petal is
detached. One falls not far from your feet,
and you notice the red spot in the snow.

The color sparkles in the sunlight, catching
your curious eye. No beast stands in sight;

there is nothing to fear, so you dare retrieve the lone petal. The touch of temptation is velvet against your thumb. It carries a scent you bring to your nose, and both eyes close to float on a cloud of perfume.

As your lashes lift, another scarlet drop stains the snow, at a near distance. A glance around perceives no danger, and so your footprints scar the snowflakes to retrieve another rosy leaflet as soft and sweet as the first. Your eyes shine with flecks of golden greed at the discovery of more discarded petals, and you blame the wind for scattering them mere footprints apart. All you want is a few, so you step and snatch, step and snatch, step and snatch.

Soon, there is enough velvet to rub against your cheek like a silken kerchief. Your collection of one-plus-one-more reeks of floral essence.

Distracted, you jump at the sight of the beast in your path. He stands before his lair, grinning without love. His callous hands grip at thorns on a single naked stem, and you look down at your own hands that now cup his rose. But how can it be?

You would never take a rose from a beast. You would shrink from the gift and refuse it. He knows that is what you would do.

October 2nd

Temptations don't appear nearly as harmful as the roads they lead you down.

October 3rd

Your weaknesses may not seem overwhelming, but they'll create the biggest problems you'll ever face.

October 4th

Fear is the devil's most powerful tool because he can't always convince a good man to do wrong, but he can paralyze his will with fright, keeping a good man from doing what is right. It eventually results in the same end.

October 5th

Discouragement, fear, and depression—
three villains who lurk in the dark.
They slip inside souls with a blindfold and
goals to shatter your dreams and
extinguish your spark.

Their tactics are highly effective.
They crush a great many each day.
And under their spell it is easy to dwell on
fiascoes and failures that end in dismay.

The heart and the mind are left heavy.
The last speck of will is erased.
And nothing stays on when these villains
are gone but a mouthful of bile with the
bitterest taste.

Alas! You must conquer the scoundrels!
Elude, dodge, and keep them at bay!
To feel fear slink in, boring under your
skin, is a sign that his brothers are well on
their way.

So reach for your weapons against them!
Take hope and hard work in each hand!
Strap faith on your hips and a prayer on
your lips, and show those debasers how
firmly you stand!

Discouragement, fear and depression;
the truth should be known of these cads.
They're empty and weak; it is your
strength they seek. Deny them and life is
your wish in the bag.

October 6th

It is my belief that almost anyone can be
had with breadcrumbs. For if you leave a
trail of the right variety, your prey will
come straight to you.

October 7th

A princess once carefully kissed a
porcupine to be kind, upon which he began
to think himself a prince. He then dressed
like a prince, behaved like a prince, and

announced himself to be a prince. The world, therefore, saw him as such, and so a porcupine prince he was. (Of course, most were reluctant to argue with him otherwise.)

October 8th

Anyone who looks good with a bald head is seriously sexy.

October 9th

What would it be like to live as a butterfly, being admired by the world for your color and beauty and grace? What would it be like to live as a spider, having people shriek and jump and throw a shoe at the very notice of you?
I have tasted both—looks of desire and repulsion.
How sad it is that we judge a life by such a trivial thing as appearance.

October 10th

"Physical attractiveness is no indicator of an individual's beauty."

—from *'The Beauty of Ugh'*

October 11th

My pain builds like storm clouds—massive, dark, and heavy with teardrops. Moisture falls torrential as if my world is a violent, eternal downpour; however, at long last the source runs dry and the bitter storm does cease. Blue skies dare to glow where the gloom has dissipated. I breathe it in, hoping to cleanse my inner soul. A laden heart tells me the truth; the clear sky is an illusion. Old pain rushes back like a flood, providing means for clouds to form and expand once again until it is too much to bear and the heaviness turns to rain.
I cannot find refuge from this woe.
It is my never-ending heartache.

October 12th

If you couldn't sense heat, you'd not be
alive. And if that heat never grew
uncomfortable, you would never move.
And if you were stagnant—unchallenged
by unpredictable flares—you would never
grow capable of shielding yourself from
harsher flames. So yes, life was meant to
drag you straight through the fire.

October 13th

A moment of torture feels like an eternity,
while an eternity of joy passes in a
moment. Perhaps time is naught but an
illusion.

October 14th

A great many problems could be solved by
nothing more than a change in thinking.

October 15th

The louder you bellyache, the longer your stomach will hurt.

October 16th

Be careful what you wish for. It may turn out that making the wish was the only good part.

October 17th

"Despair is not for the living
but for those unable to rise and continue;
they are the only souls with a right to it.
It is an end where breath and strength and
will have vanished, leaving no way to
persevere.
To sink into the abyss that is despair
is to suffer an existence far worse than
death; therefore, cling to its enemy, our
ally—hope.
For life goes on, and we must not live in
despair.
We must not."

—from *'Eena, The Two Sisters'*

October 18th

Punishing a person for the wrongs of another makes about as much sense as throwing up to enjoy the meal a second time.

October 19th

It's silly to think the left eye would envy the right or that one foot would be jealous of the other, and yet so often it is the case.

October 20th

"Enemies may unite to eliminate a common threat, but never without a wary eye fixed on their ally."

—from *'The Tarishe Curse'*

October 21st

One bad turn does not excuse another.

October 22nd

"Vengeance would have us assault an enemy's pride to beat him down. But vengeance hides a dangerous truth, for a humbled foe gains patience, courage, strength, and greater determination."

—from *'The Tarishe Curse'*

October 23rd

Before you take that first curious, coerced, spiteful, or vengeful step forward, remember this: it's a thousand times easier to slip into a muddy pit than it is to climb out of one.

October 24th

"A monster's worst fear is of being found."

—from *'Secrets of a Noble Key Keeper'*

October 25th

Lies don't fit snugly into disguises.
Eventually the cloak falls off and you're
left staring at the naked truth which is
always an uncomfortable situation.

October 26th

A liar deceives himself more than anyone,
for he believes he can remain a person of
good character when he cannot.

October 27th

Life is a walk through the forest.
Don't fear the trees; fear what lurks behind
them.

October 28ᵗʰ

Dress the part! Invent and pretend to your
heart's content! Act, sing, and dance
while everyone's watching! The world's a
stage, remember?

October 29ᵗʰ

It wasn't a kiss that changed the frog, but
the fact that a young girl looked beneath
warts and slime and believed she saw a
prince. So he became one.

October 30ᵗʰ

Haunt an old house.
Ask for a treat.
Laugh like a witch.
Lick something sweet.
Offer a trick.
Wander a maze.
Echo a boo.
Exclaim the phrase—
Normal's unnatural on Halloween!

October 31st

The Harvest Moon glows round and bold,
in pumpkin shades outlined in gold,
illuminating eerie forms,
unnatural as a candied corn.
Beware what dare crawls up your sleeve,
for 'tis the night called Hallows Eve.

NOVEMBER

Family gathers
to share good noise and good food.
Gratitude abounds.

November 1st

The earth provides us a brand new
beginning every twenty-four hours. It is a
repeated invitation to breathe in the cool
morning air and start afresh; to mimic the
sunrise and brighten up while reaching
once more for the sky; to carry a glad song
in our heart like the early birds; and, as
faithfully as the morning dew, to wash off
the dust from yesterday.

November 2nd

Having this, we want that.
Owning some, we want more.
Standing here, we wish to be there.
If it's impossible, we struggle to make it
happen.

Why are we like this? Why not be content with some, here, and now? Why is enough not enough?

Because humans are ambitious creatures not meant to be idle or fruitless. We strive to learn, to grow, to achieve, to amass; therefore, we will never be content.

November 3rd

Humans are forever discontent—always thinking there are better alternatives to their present circumstances.

November 4th

The sign of a good leader is easy to recognize, though it is hardly ever seen. For the greatest leaders are those who share as equals in the trials and struggles, the demands and expectations, the hills and trenches, the laws and punishments placed upon the backs of those governed. A great leader is motivated not by power but by compassion. Therefore he can do nothing but make himself a servant to those whom he rules. Such a leader is unequivocally respected, and loved for loving.

November 5ᵗʰ

It is a fact that one man can be deliriously happy in the exact situation that causes another man to wither from depression.

November 6ᵗʰ

When thunderstorms roll in, you make a choice to either succumb with tears to the gloomy downpour, or smile and look for rainbows.

November 7ᵗʰ

Changing your attitude, your outlook, your mindset, perspective, disposition, or mood—they all mean controlling where you allow your thoughts to linger.

November 8th

Happiness found me alone one day and
took me by the hand.
He showed me how the sun gave out its
warmth across the land.
Sadness found me content and smiling
upward at the sun.
He talked of droughts and blindness and
what burning rays had done.

Happiness found me alone again and
pointed to the sky.
He showed me how the storms created
rainbows way up high.
Sadness found me intrigued and took me
to the rainbow's end.
He showed me how it disappeared to ne'er
return again.

Happiness found me alone and taught me
how to sing a song.
He sang a dozen melodies as I chirped
right along.
Sadness found me singing out and covered
up his ears.
He said the noise was deafening, and
wished he couldn't hear.

Happiness found me alone and gave me
seven coins of gold.
He showed me many fancy things that
merchants often sold.
Sadness found me admiring the pretty
things I'd bought.
He pointed out my empty purse and money
I had not.

Happiness found me alone and helped me
talk to someone new.
He called the boy my friend and said that I
was his friend too.
Sadness found me together with my kind,
attentive friend.
He whispered of betrayal and how broken
hearts don't mend.

Happiness found me alone and held me
tight in his embrace.
He whispered kindness in my ear and
kissed me on the face.
Sadness found me with Happiness but
before he spoke at all,
I told him he'd have better luck at talking
to the wall.

November 9th

I love happy people; they're like smile magnets.

November 10th

Music is my enchanter, the seducer of my emotions, the fire and ice that moves me.

November 11th

So you had a bad day. Kick it aside and be grateful for one less bad day to pass through.

November 12th

"If we were always given a choice as to every path presented us in life, a multitude of roads leading to priceless treasures would forever go untraveled.
Be grateful for your adversities.
From toil and triumph evolves a life worth living."

—from *'Brahna A'Mahr'*

November 13th

Just like salt makes sweet taste sweeter,
trials make happy feel happier.

November 14th

"Life is too hard to maintain a constantly
serious outlook. You have to laugh at
yourself and the world now and then—see
humor in undesirable circumstances, even
harsh situations—or you will either rot
from the inside or go stark-raving mad.
Humor is power against the worst
oppression. It lightens heavy burdens; it
allows one to smile while in agony; it
eases excruciating pains. In short, humor
makes the intolerable tolerable."

—from *'Smile Anyway'*

November 15th

Like the grand eagle, you spread your
wings
and put forth the effort to do great things.
Looking skyward you dared to challenge
the wind,

harnessing power to help you ascend.

With an eye on the goal, fixed in flight,
you climbed to an impressive height.
Undaunted by gusts and unkind gales,
you never gave up and would not fail.

So now you've reached where few even
try,
as the eagle high in a glorious sky.
Not superior, but grand.
Not proud, but sure.
Not a cub, wolf, or bear but an eagle pure.
Today you soar.

November 16th

Like yeast, it's impressive how
considerably an ounce of determination
can make one's efforts grow and expand.

November 17th

Something wonderful is about to happen,
and something awful is about to happen.
You can dwell on either one.
It's your choice.

November 18th

There are many pitfalls in life; one is
dwelling on blame.
It's pointless. Move on.

November 19th

Problems don't actually exist. They're just
the hallucinogenic effects of people being
weirded out on what they think life is
supposed to be.

November 20th

There is peculiar magic in kindness.
I know. I've seen its strange spell at work.
As a grade-schooler I was always
picked on to some degree, singled out
because of my high IQ and short stature.
But the worst day of my young life was
when Derek Meyer moved into town and
parked himself in the seat behind mine in
Mrs. Stanford's fourth grade classroom.
Apparently I had a bull's eye painted on
the back of my head because from that

very moment, finding things to pitch at me became his obsession.

It was a week into what had become a swat-and-duck match when I found his husky shadow eclipsing my own. I was on my way home from school. Up to then, Derek had limited his bullying to school grounds. A jolt of sheer terror shot through me when he jeeringly chanted my name, threatening to throw a rock directly between my shoulder blades—a good-sized nugget he was lobbing from one fat hand to the other.

I tried to hustle along, wanting to reach home quickly, yet fearing what might happen if he discovered the location of my house. I was doing a hasty speed-walk when the first stone whizzed by my head and kicked up a cloud of dirt only a yard in front of me. I couldn't help but gawk over my shoulder, a horrific picture of shock and fear entangling my expression.

I was ordered to run if I didn't care to eat stone soup for dinner. And so I ran….for my life. Entirely true to the bully creed, Derek didn't show any mercy. He ran after me, pitching jagged rocks at my legs. Those that hit burned like bee stings. I prayed for deliverance as well as the ability to keep from tripping over raining stones.

Funny thing how prayers sometimes come in the form of regular kids.

Lenny Dover wasn't anyone extraordinary, but he wasn't known for harassing anyone either. It was his unfittingly enthusiastic voice and an odd comment that paused the granite shower.

"Dang, Derek! You've one wicked arm! You play any ball?"

Curious, I turned to look, still scuttling backwards. Lenny spoke to me next, halting my attempt at escape.

"Hey, Daisy, hold up! I bet you'd have a heckuva time hitting a home run with him pitching, don't you think?"

Astounded by the fact that he seemed to expect me to participate in a conversation with this Neanderthal, I said nothing.

Lenny went right on talking to the bully, smiling the whole time as if they were good pals. He bragged about my swinging arm and how I hit more home runs than anyone else on our softball team. He got Derek to demonstrate a fast pitch with the remaining rocks in his hands—

this time the target was a skinny tree and not me. An eager sales pitch ensued whereby Lenny gradually convinced my tormentor that he was the next Walter Johnson, and that he shouldn't let his talent go to waste. By the time they were done talking, Lenny had Derek chomping at the bit to join our softball team.

"Derek's gonna have one lightning-fast curve ball with that arm of his, ain't he, Daisy?"

One corner of my mouth forced a bleak smile. I still couldn't voice a reply in my dazed state. The big bully gave Lenny a high five. He smiled at me without malice. And then he did the craziest thing; he apologized for all the harassment—said he was just playing around. He even called me a good sport.

What the...?

I watched Derek turn and head back toward the schoolyard. When Lenny started in the direction of my house, I chased after him.

"Why in the heck did you do that?" I snapped. "I don't want that stupid bully on our softball team!"

"Sure you do," Lenny insisted. "He really does have a good arm."

"Yeah, I'm painfully aware of that."
I was sure bruises were forming on my
legs where rocks had pelted me. "I wish
you'd thrown a big boulder at Derek's
head."

"Nah. You don't really wish that."

"Yes I do! The guy's a jerk! He's
mean to me every day, for no reason at
all!"

Lenny glanced my way and grinned
shrewdly. "He won't be mean to you
anymore."

"Why? What do you mean?"

Lenny stopped walking to spell out
just how ingeniously he'd saved me from
Derek, not just this once but every day in
the future.

"If I had picked a fight with the guy,
tomorrow he'd be seeking revenge on both
of us. Now, instead, he'll be handing you
a bat, wanting to play ball. Look, Daisy,
it's like my dad once told me, *people have
a hard time being unkind to you when they
think you admire them.* Derek now thinks
we admire him."

I gawked at my genius hero.

"You're welcome," he winked.

"Yeah, whatever......thanks."

Strangely enough, Derek and I actually became decent friends after that. Like I said—there is peculiar magic in kindness.

November 21st

I wish upon a glimmering star,
My hopes as distant and as far.
So if this wish does not come true,
I'm thankful for the few that do.

November 22nd

For things I am not thankful for—experiences I would never volunteer to relive—I recognize how they have changed me. My depth of compassion and humility, the sincerity of my empathy and understanding, and the duration of my patience have all been refined by bitter suffering. I thank God for the lessons learned. I am a better person for it, but I still abhor those awful trials.

November 23rd

Theories look great on paper until reality
scribbles all over the page.

November 24th

Words that should cross your lips with
ease: thank you, love you, sorry, please.

November 25th

I wish the hearts of human beings pumped
with kind desires.
I wish every gaze landed on the eyes of
others compassionately.
I wish hatred, envy, and vengeance were
alien concepts to humankind.
I wish the precious worth of every soul
was universally understood.

November 26th

The richest people are those who have an abundance of what we take with us into the next life.

November 27th

There are those who fear the sunset, worried they will never see light again. There are those who ignore the sunrise, squandering dawn, believing they will never run out of daylight. And then there are those who have learned to live in the sun's warmth, gauging time by its positions, thankful at night that the day happened. Be aware of time. Use it wisely. Be thankful for the light allotted.

November 28th

I walk at night under a moonless sky. Only the terrain guides my steps, yet my footfall is as sure as if a dozen suns lit the way. I go to meet you under a leafless tree that never seems to grow or alter its shape. I am uncertain if it still lives or has learned to disguise its death. The same thought crosses my mind when I feel your cold fingers take my hand. It is not the tree I reflect upon.

'Do you still love me?' The words tumble clumsily out of the dark.

Hesitation is its own answer, but I reply anyway, *'I'm here,'* as if my words were whispered comfort and not a weathered blade. They are taken wrong.

'I love you too.'

Your arms wrap me up and clamp tightly around my waist. An old, familiar kiss hardens my lips. I wonder why it is I return to this place every year where only memories remain fond. Perhaps it is because I keep hoping this leafless tree will either change or die.

November 29th

My life is a fairytale stuck at the climax.

November 30th

I had hit a low point in life.

It wasn't exactly rock bottom, more like being suspended above it within foot reach. Life had become a chore; opening my eyes every morning was work. Over a period of months I'd developed the desperate habit of praying for tender mercies before attempting the arduous task of facing the day. Had it not been for a few individuals who relied upon me, I may not have bothered.

At daybreak I began counting down the minutes until bedtime. I longed for those hours of darkness when sleep numbed my troubled mind. My morning routine was exercise, but I forced myself by saying, "Just do one more thing," followed by the same mental push, "Just one more thing."

My problems amounted to many. I felt buried beneath them, wedged tight inside fixed circumstances. I wanted to change things—my life, my outlook, myself—but every attempt seemed like grasping at straws with nothing to cling to. I was depressed and despairing. Life was misery.

One day something small happened.

It wasn't the individual who spoke to me, for it could have been anyone. It was no physical act of love or rescue. Nor was there any acknowledgement that he could see me drowning internally. He simply appeared, glowing like human sunshine. There was a radiance about him, invisible but for the painted smile on his face.

He said hello.
He told me I looked as pretty as always.
He pointed out the beautiful day and mentioned how lucky we were to be blessed by so many days of sunshine.

Simple, kind words.

The entire time his gaze was locked on mine, his eyes bright and smiling. He was seeing me, not my physical shell but the person housing it—the *me* inside. In those few moments, I felt my deflated spirit expand as if he'd breathed life back into it.

Most likely when he turned and walked away it was without any awareness of the effect his focused attention had had on me. I'd been helped in a real way. Not healed, but ministered to. I've come to realize after contemplation that sometimes what we need is a Good Samaritan to perform CPR on our spirits.

DECEMBER

Twinkle tiny star.
Oh, how great you truly are!
God's sign from afar.

December 1st

The sweetest melody that plays
on starry nights and wintry days,
most soothing to my listening ears
and calming to beleaguering fears,
I call a symphony on air—
the song of sweet, still silence rare.

December 2nd

I can and will improve the world.
I will smile, show kindness, and be
grateful.
I refuse to be unhappy.

December 3rd

The only way to change the world is to quit thinking it's a job for Superman. Real power lies in your own hands.

December 4th

Your efforts extend like ripples on the ocean, much further than you know.

December 5th

There are times you find yourself standing by the wayside, watching as someone struggles to dig a well with a spoon, and you wish with all your heart you had arms and a shovel.

December 6th

You are here to make a difference, to either improve the world or worsen it. And whether or not you consciously choose to, you will accomplish one or the other.

December 7th

You cannot fully understand a person's need until you have endured the same need. As hard as you may try to predict and comprehend their situation and suffering, I guarantee you'll fall short until you've been there.

December 8th

The humanitarian is a treasure hunter seeking gems of remedy and appreciation.

December 9th

The denial of assistance is sometimes the greatest assistance. The trick is recognizing when this is the case.

December 10th

It seems a peculiar thing when I go to fill my own cup; it remains empty as if the liquid evaporates as soon as it touches the glass. Yet when I reach to top off the cups of others, my own spills over. This is the crazy magic of charity.

December 11th

An accumulation of pennies is a fortune. Day-to-day practice is perfection. A dream realized is nothing more than many steps taken toward the borders of once-impossible.

December 12th

A thought can prompt. Words can stir. But it takes action to attain a dream.

December 13th

There are two kinds of people in this world: those who follow the popular majority, and those who possess good sense. In other words, you can either let the crowd steer you right over a cliff, or you can stop to peer beyond the brink and see how a fall will likely end in tragedy.

December 14th

It is to our own detriment that we underestimate the might of small and simple things.

December 15th

Helpful is happy.
Selfish is sad.
(It's not uncommon to confuse the two.)

December 16th

Why must you know the details of my troubles to have compassion? Is it not enough to show compassion simply because you know that everyone has troubles?

December 17th

Do we ignore the needy
to spite the greedy?
Or share and defend
despite those who pretend?

December 18th

You don't do kind deeds expecting
kindness in return. You don't do kind
deeds because you deem the recipient
worthy. You do kind deeds because it's
who you are, and because you understand
the powerful difference your gentle hand
makes in this dreary world.

December 19th

If people were kinder, the world might
cease weeping.

December 20th

I believe life is an education meant to
teach us the need to be better people. And
I believe this learning often takes place
through trial and error which may mean
being an awful person at times before
clearly seeing and grasping the necessity to
change. If you don't agree with me, just
ask Mr. Ebenezer Scrooge. I think Charles
Dickens got it quite right.

December 21st

It is in the coldest months that hugs linger snug, and they warm the soul the most.

December 22nd

It was early in the morning, three days before Christmas. I was in bed with my eyes closed, struggling to decide if my latest dream was less or more reality. I had retired to bed late the previous night, having stayed up to wrap gifts and watch *It's a Wonderful Life* all by my lonesome while the rest of the house snored peacefully in the background. I had wept emotionally over George's realization that the world was a better place with him alive. Then I'd turned off the TV and gone to bed.

Years ago when my children were young, viewing this holiday classic had been an annual tradition. But ever since my four darlings had entered puberty, they'd unanimously agreed it was more torture than treat to watch a black-and-white rerun of some crazy, old, dead guy......no matter how many tears it cost their mother. My husband had sided with the majority—a little too eagerly—so I now upheld the holiday ritual alone.

Still in bed, I opened my eyes and stared up at a ceiling that resembled muddy tapioca. The grogginess had lifted enough for me to realize I'd been dreaming, but the impact I felt from those realistic visions bothered me. Sometime in the night I'd assimilated George Baily's experience into my subconscious, and I'd become a ghost in my own home, invisible to my husband and four children. I was painfully aware of them but unable to interact with anyone. Though I stood directly in their path, they were entirely oblivious of me.

The worst part wasn't my sudden ghostliness. Nor was it the fact that I couldn't communicate with the ones I loved. What weighed heavy on my heart in the dream—and now while awake—was the fact that my family didn't appear the least bit troubled by my absence. No one had stopped for even a second to question where I was, to call out my name or expend the slightest amount of effort searching the house for me. They simply went on with their daily routines, engrossed in whatever selfish activities each had planned for the day.

No one missed me. It was disheartening.

The fact that my entire family had opted out of movie night the evening prior only made my condition graver. I may as well have been a real ghost for as little as I was wanted. In truth, every other soul in the house was capable of taking care of him or herself; my family could go right on functioning without me.

My goal as a parent had always been to teach each child to be self-sufficient and independent; so I had succeeded. That was good! But I felt miserable nonetheless.

Pulling the covers over my head, I curled up into a ball and fell back asleep, depressed and envious of the fact that Bedford Falls had fallen apart without George Baily.

I was jolted awake—startled upright. A glance at the clock showed I'd overslept by a couple hours. Five unsmiling faces surrounded my bed, all focused on me. I realized it was my youngest daughter squawking, *"Moth—er!"* that had awakened me. The silence accompanying four tight stares only lasted long enough for me to wipe at the mascara I imagined was smeared beneath my eyes.

"What are you all…?" I started, only to be drowned out by sibling teens talking at once.

"Mother, I need a ride to Joslin's house—stupid 'Big Foot' won't take me."

"Because I can't, Bratilda. I told you, I'm scheduled to work…"

"So drop me off first….Mother, tell him!"

"Mom, I'm short on cash, and I need gas money…"

"No, no, no way! He hasn't done one chore around here; I've been doing everything!"

"Forget them—I really need some money, Mom. We're Christmas shopping at the mall…"

"Hey, Ma, did you get my red sweater washed? You said you'd have it ready for my concert tonight…"

"Mom, please tell me you are not going to make me go to his dork concert tonight! I have that Christmas cookie exchange—you said you'd help me make sugar cookies today…"

Just then, my husband squeezed his head in. *"Hunny? Have you seen my car keys anywhere?"*

If in reality I were to wake up and find myself a ghost, this beautiful family of mine would probably find a way to function. But my dream had been wrong. My family needed me, even if I was slightly taken for granted. The truth felt radiant and clear—Bedford Falls was in chaos. Good old George Bailey's wonderful life had nothing on mine.

December 23rd

The greatest gift you can give is your time. Not money, not items, not food, not pretty cards with handwritten sentiment, but time. People need your presence. The way you can help a soul the most is to simply be there.

December 24th

Christmas is a whisper of peace and a sigh of hope on the lips of love.

December 25th

Christ was born in Bethlehem as
Heaven sang with joy.
Roaming shepherds came to see the
Infant, swaddled boy.
Several wise men sought him out,
Traveling from afar.
Mary wondered, looking skyward
At a bright, new star.
Sacred was the Christ child's birth.
Sacred is **CHRISTMAS**.

December 26th

The happiest adults are those who never
buried old toys or abandoned imaginary
friends.

December 27th

I love snowflakes simply for the reason
that each one is unique; non-identical to
zillions of crystalized counterparts. It's a
difficult notion to wrap your brain around,
and yet it reminds me that amidst the
innumerable stories told throughout the

ages, a distinctly new one rests on the tip
of an author's pen.

December 28th

You will find there are times you must
grasp your life with both hands and
forcefully steer it in a new direction and
then strain to hold your course until the
storms of fear, weakness, and doubt abate.

December 29th

It's been a harsh fight.
You've been pummeled and knocked
down. Your body aches, flesh torn and
bruised. Your eyes can hardly see through
a stream of blood. But you are cognizant
and alive; therefore, you rise from the
fight.

This is life. It will test your will, your
strength, and endurance. It will challenge
your faith and convictions. It will scar
your hopes and try your beliefs. In the
end, life validates those who refuse to stay
down.

December 30th

> Minutes turn into hours
> that add up to days
> amounting to weeks
> that become months
> melting into years
> accumulating for decades
> to pile up for centuries
> and ultimately form minutes again—
> just on a grander, divine scale.

December 31st

> In constant view keeps mightily true an
> honest resolve to do.

"*All truth starts out as a wish; hence,*

reality is born from fairytale."
- Richelle E. Goodrich, '**My Aquarius**'

ABOUT THE AUTHOR

Richelle E. Goodrich is native to the Pacific Northwest, born in Utah but raised in Washington State. She lives with her husband and three boys somewhere in a compromise between city and country settings. Richelle graduated from Eastern Washington University with bachelor's degrees in Liberal Studies and Natural Science / Mathematics Education. She loves the arts—drama, sketching, painting, literature—and writes whenever opportunity presents itself. This author describes herself beautifully in the following quote:

"I like bubbles in everything. I respect the power of silence. In cold or warm weather, I favor a mug of hot cocoa. I admire cats—their autonomy, grace, and mystery. I awe at the fiery colors in a sunset. I believe in deity. I hear most often with my eyes, and I will trust a facial expression before any accompanying comment. I invent rules, words, adventures, and imaginary friends. I pretend something wonderful every day. I will never quit pretending."

-Richelle E. Goodrich

DANDELIONS:
The Disappearance of Annabelle Fancher

By Richelle E. Goodrich

What does a child do when life hurts? She dreams up a hero.
~ A childhood trial of survival.
~ Realism and fantasy beautifully intertwined.

This fictional tale is a suspenseful, human-interest account detailing the harsh reality endured by young Anna. It tenderly acquaints the reader with a lonely young girl and shares her courage facing adversity. Many of the events were taken from the lives of actual people.

Annabelle Fancher lives with her mother and her often-absent, alcoholic father. When he's not on the road, his presence at home instills heightened anxiety in his wife and daughter—fear caused by years of drunken cruelty. Annabelle copes with her circumstances by escaping into storybooks where she dreams characters to life from popular fairytales. There in her dreams she manages to form make-believe moments of happiness.

School is the only place she interacts socially, where a few individuals suspecting her circumstances attempt to reach out to the quiet child; however, it is an imagined friend whom she turns to repeatedly for comfort and kindness. But when his ghostly form appears during waking hours—his voice augmenting the hallucination—it becomes a struggle for Annabelle to keep reality and pretend from blurring boundaries. Her choice, it seems, is to happily succumb to madness or embrace her cruel reality.

SECRETS OF A NOBLE KEY KEEPER
~ The Story of Dreamland ~

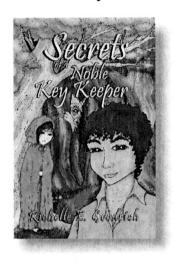

By Richelle E. Goodrich

There are things
that make no sense,
that seem unreal,
that can't be grasped
or understood
or explained,
that maybe don't even exist…
And still, somehow, those wonderful things touch and
change our lives.
Isn't it strange?

Meet a curious, young man whose calling it is to guard the gates of his homeland. As key keeper of Dreamland, Gavin comes across many outsiders referred to by his people as dreamers. Through a variety of bizarre and creative antics, Gavin steers these roaming trespassers away from the borders of his magical world—a world where ogres bowl for their dinner, and pirates sail the clouds to plunder diamonds from the night's sky, and bubbleberries make a person burp out loud. It is a place where anything imaginable is commonplace.

All the while, the young key keeper finds himself increasingly intrigued by stories of the outside world. Snooping about, he is captivated by a dreamer who peaks his interest in the ordinary.

This book is supplemental to *Dandelions: The Disappearance of Annabelle Fancher*

CPSIA information can be obtained
at www.ICGtesting.com
Printed in the USA
FFOW02n1713210316
22506FF